For my enablers, be they afraid or infatuated. My thanks to Calum McGee for lending your eyes, Ariadne Flavell for lending your ears, and Pema Clark for your wisdom.

And most importantly, for my mum.

May we all come to live in better times.

Copyright © 2021 Amie M Marie
Mandells House Publishing
www.amiemarie.co.uk

First paperback edition in February 2021

ISBN 978-1-8383769-0-1 (paperback)
ISBN 978-1-8383769-1-8 (ebook)

Cover Art by Emma Jane Betts
@ EmmaJaneBetts4

Foreword by Alec S Mann
Contributions from Pema Clark, Conér Swords, David McCabe Jr, and Eliott Simpson

Performance rights and actor scripts of Emperor May & A Play About Theresa May are available through Cyberpress's site: www.StagePlays.com, or by email admin@stageplays.com

The Internet Theatre Bookshop
3 Dudley Court
YORK
YO31 8LR

Most requests for modification such as cutting lines or scenes will be accepted, however these must be put in writing to the aforementioned site prior to performance. Otherwise productions run the risk of breaching copyright.

Performance rights are required whether or not an audience pays admission. The only time the scripts may be performed without charge is in a private home, for audition, or in a classroom.

THE PLAY ABOUT THERESA MAY

Foreword

I am Amie's fiancée for a reason. She might be the dumbest smart person I have ever met, who can fit into every job or theatrical role as if she were born to it, but can't do the washing up. Her dishes are as dirty as a Tory donor.

I met Amie in 2015 during the third year of my degree, while extremely drunk at a party. I have very little memory of that night but apparently I gave a lot of people a lot of advice. We worked together a number of times over the next year, and I came to value her opinion on virtually anything. We were both studying scriptwriting, but had ambitions beyond the university. I founded a theatre company, and Amie was one of my most valued creative contributors. Even if I was never fully prepared for her contributions.

She is the most politically aware person I have ever met and her approach to politics (especially through the lens of theatre) fascinates me. She has written several plays grounded in this arena, but none quite like this. Over the course of the 2010s, the Conservative administration has a number of greatest hits: the demonisation of foreigners and the EU, the greater transfer of wealth to the rich, the shredding of public services, and many more, creating a wealth of material to explore.

Theresa May, however, I consider a footnote. Not known, like Cameron, for fucking up a referendum, nor, like Johnson, for fucking up a pandemic. What did May *do* that was of note? I cannot answer that, but Amie can, and I value her opinion. I have never seen a play that managed to portray the ineptitude, the ignorance, the viciousness, of this administration and yet somehow this is still a comedy...?

Amie thrives on theatrical anarchy, yet can construct entire plays set in rigid rhythmic metre. She gives characters a voice, even though she hates them. She sends out a coherent and concise message, but adores creating confusion. I do not know what you will get out of reading this play, but you will not end it as the same person who began. Even if you just become confused.

Good luck,

Alec S Mann
Stage & Screen writer
Director of Bottled Spider Productions

Preface

I first encountered Amie Marie's A Play About Theresa May in its development at the University of East Anglia and encouraged its future life due to its timely and inventive satire on the government at the time. One of the great things about it was that the writing grew out of the writer-actor's depth of research and ability to find an even more charismatic version of the Prime Minister than existed on television. This was part of its charm and it was exactly what we needed to see in the wake of May's battle with coming up with a Brexit deal that was, ultimately, rejected. In its further development, the addition of the Queen and Donald Trump along with Macron and Johnson, amongst others, was a deft move and served to flesh out the satire with precision and a keen eye for current affairs.

Amie's characters are bigger than life and serve to voice what we were all thinking at the time when Brexit seemed to go on ad nauseam in the popular press. She brings up everything not to like about the Conservative government at the time: the handling of Grenfell, the Windrush scandal, wealth inequality and taxes. Without underplaying any of these deeply troubling subjects, she offers up a scathingly comedic portrayal of Theresa May and her handling of Brexit with a finely tuned hand for comedy.

Pema Clark PhD
Associate Tutor
UEA Drama

Image description: Amie costumed as Theresa May with grey wig, blue jacket, chunky necklace, and make up which ages her significantly.

Comedy As Responsibility

Comedy is a remarkably powerful tool in that it has the ability to both inform and alter public opinion. A joke is like a puzzle with a point of view; the joke teller lays out the clues then, once the audience solves the puzzle, they laugh as if to affirm that the joke has been realised and that they agree with the point of view being expressed.

Even a well constructed joke can still fail to utter a laugh if it's expressing views that are universally considered abhorrent. But with enough wit, relatability, repetition, subtext or any other manner of techniques, you can convince an audience to agree with almost any viewpoint. The sensation of laughter is one which we instinctively crave because of the satisfying feelings it grants us, so naturally our minds sway to think positively of those who grant us such feelings. This is where comedy becomes one of the most powerful tools imaginable.

Through humour and a platform, you possess the power to influence people's opinions through delivering mirth. History has shown how such power can be used for both sides of the moral spectrum, both for promoting harmful stereotypes, and for exposing the tyranny and hypocrisy of those who rule. Through this we see how comedy has a transformative nature in its ability to influence others, but it's potential for causing harm or healing matters entirely upon who uses it.

Comedy can be used to spread either hate and ridicule or tolerance and love; dependant entirely upon what subject the mockery is aimed towards. Therefore the ability to bring joy and laughter to others is more than just a privilege, but a moral responsibility.

In a world where division is one of the greatest enablers of corruption and injustice, the question we must ask ourselves is not why we laugh, but who we are laughing at and who we are laughing with.

Eliott Simpson
Autistic & Asexual Comedian
Videographer, Film Editor, & Transcriptionist

Introduction

The Play About Theresa May is an indignant reply to Conservative injustice focusing on May's 1106 days in power.

On her 293rd day, I had the opportunity to share a ten minute political performance with my theatre cohort at the University of East Anglia. Rather than delving into political concepts or head-butting with individual laws and policy changes, it seemed reasonable to begin at the top, with the very face of modern UK politics: the Prime Minister.

What began as a short political satire on the frustrating hypocrisy and two-faced sound-bite nature of Theresa May's Premiership snowballed into a larger, faster, more convoluted stage play.

And it already began as a pretty fast-talking convoluted stage play.

Since David Cameron had scarpered off, dropping the Brexit hot potato from his delicate, DLA-ripping hands, May had entered the scene as a crocodile-tear Thatcher-wannabe glass-cliff fall guy. Her well-written so-called "radical" opening statement as Prime Minster was infuriating in all the ways it gracefully smoothed over her ugly history: as racist "hostile environment" Home Secretary and as a pro-war, anti-welfare MP.

It was a stroke of genius from her speech writers: admitting that inequality exists in such a way that no one is to blame, angering no one, and also promising nothing.

Her team began in earnest to pump out three and four word slogans. Mottos. Mantras. Catchphrases. Things to distract the public, things that sound positive, shallow things, to take advantage of the busy and economically-fragile lifestyle of UK residents doing their best to keep afloat as poverty rises and workers' rights fall. As Home Secretary, Theresa May was directly responsible for the "hostile environment" culture, of systemically assuming foreign-looking means law-breaking no-gooder and rushed deportations. Her government was approving weapon licences to countries actively breaking human rights or fighting in undeclared wars. Her government continued the trend of increased corporate welfare but slashing citizen's welfare. She began a long-overdue consultation into Gender Recognition Act reform recklessly, hoping to have a second LGBT+ win in recent history by improving things for Trans people, only to stir up the worst transphobic hate and rhetoric in memory, birthing dozens of influential genital-obsessed anti-science hate-groups.

It is worth pausing to reflect that Theresa May was a glass cliff.

Where a glass ceiling is an invisible barrier, and a glass elevator is an invisible streamline to the top, a glass cliff is to be elevated up high in order to take the fall.

Theresa May was the fall guy for David Cameron's Brexit. She was the one that the problems of the Conservative government and their Brexit arrangement *had* to stick it to. She knew this and she martyred herself for her ideology. Of one Conservative nation.

To this day, I do not forgive Theresa May for her part in history and all she harmed.

I have not fallen into the trap of sympathy for her. Her choices, whether active or complicit, has killed people. Has impoverished people. Has disabled people. She brought in hate crime and budget cuts, closed down libraries and job centres, cheapened schools and undermined global efforts for peace and climate resolution.

While she continued on the track David Cameron made, I hold her to blame for her actions - as well as holding him responsible for his. Our gender matching is no reason to minimise or dismiss the repercussions and consequences of her term.

She is not a weak woman.

She is a cruel woman.

30 Days Left / Emperor May // Puppet of Warlords /// an Imperial, Empirical Bitch

Written by Amie M Marie

First performed 2nd May 2017.

Image description: Amie dressed in red jacket and pink skirt as Theresa May, with a grey wig and aged make up. Behind her, on the screen, is a recording of Amie as Carol Duffy, with long curly black hair.

An austere stage, no furniture or props, except for a flat-screen TV on the far wall facing the audience.

The Prime Minister, THERESA MAY, enters in a flurry. Pauses. She is wearing a red suit jacket, red pencil skirt, black low-heel shoes: as on 27th January 2017. She reveals a bag of chips, stares into the audience, and chews strangely - as on 2nd May 2017.

A beat, and then she throws the chips across the stage and into the wings.

THERESA: In Ancient Rome, Augustus – once called Octavian – led the Romans immediately after the fall of Caesar. Augustus, seeking political security, and knowing the power of propaganda, sought the best of their contemporary wordsmiths and commissioned the greatest tale of their time. The Aeneid – a story so fantastic, so interwoven with myth and truth and lie, that the public could be fooled, ah, convinced that their leader was righteous, god given, and destined. Therefore, I, Theresa May, shall find the best of the best in Britain to deduce, amplify, and ensure my legacy. But who? We need a PR poet, a government's poet. The Poet Laureate. Carol. Carol, can you hear me?

CAROL DUFFY appears on the screen: we see her in a home office through the video call.

CAROL:	*(uncertain)* Hello, Prime Minister.
THERESA:	Carol, I have something to commission you. One can't trust the public with anything. They know nothing.
CAROL:	Isn't that why you're here, because the public voted –
THERESA:	- for Brexit, not me. Thank god, no I don't answer to them. But you see, that is what they currently think: they think that it was because of something as insignificant as our country exiting the longest and arguably greatest political peace union, with later amendments of trade deals and establishing the concept of human rights or some other such. Well, that or Cameron fucked a pig. Hard act to follow, David. But you see, this is where you come in. No, not to fuck, but to change what they think. My right to rule isn't based on the whims of a nation, like Brexit was, nor can we let it remain known that a mere 199 Tory Ministers out of 329 Tory Ministers chose me to rule all of Britain. That's 199 of a population of 64.1 million. Too small a mandate for comfort. No, we need more. Hence, you.
CAROL:	Me?
THERESA:	You.

CAROL: Me?

THERESA: Yes, you.

CAROL: Which makes two-hundred.

THERESA: What?

CAROL: So, 199 plus me makes two-hundred. Over 64.1 million. That's 0.000003% of the population.

THERESA: No, that's not right. You've misunderstood. You, as in, your talents, m'dear are needed by your Prime Minister. It's a great honour for you. You'll get to write my biography in the form of an epic poem, oh, like, say, for example – a mere example, which I'm sure you'll improve upon, - say, Virgil's Aeneid?

CAROL: I'm flattered, but, I'm not sure that you want a lesbian writing for you considering you voted against same sex marriage, Prime Minister –

THERESA: Is that too many syllables? The Prime Minister. The Primeist Minister. The Prime. Call me that from now. The Prime.

CAROL: Um, The Prime. I'm not sure I'm willing to *(interrupted)* -

THERESA: *(snapping her fingers)* Get it done.

THERESA exits.

CAROL: Get it done? Unbelievable. I'll get something done, alright. Sing to me of the woman, Muse, mad by twists and turns, Waltzing time and again off the mark, having plundered the hallowed funds for the NHS.

A pause as CAROL writes and reads back the following.

CAROL: Rosettes matching, sneeches on beaches, swapped, cycled. Politics. Courtly displays of c*untry authority, such fl*cked birds titter together, till the cat comes. Then she's hairless, skin-wrinkled sphynx, preening feathers off her maw. Opportunity. A fox, fat, feasting - celebrated with a parade of headless chickens chanting "take back control, build a fence" and swear fealty for red, white, blue faced, she - clifftop lemming – squats, vows the end of tides with their fish, seaweed, sticking sand, and coastal erosion of Great, Traditional Mud Values. She stares down the sea as it draws back Back, back. The tsunami tide but a glimmer of horizon sunlight in the bat's eye of Theresa May.

THERESA enters. She wrings her hands and hunches as she paces.

THERESA: *(Coyly)* I may have made a mistake. You need to fix it. Well, you need to make it look good.

CAROL: What?

THERESA: It is, possible, I, held hands with Trump.

THERESA retches in disgust at herself.

CAROL: What.

THERESA: It just happened. Nothing can be done, but you must, divine exactly why that was the right thing to do. In fact, everything I've ever done or will do is right. *(A mantra)* Right historically, right economically. Make Red, White, Blue Brexit a Success. I'm the Prime Minister.

CAROL: Prime Minister –

THERESA: Prime! (a pause)

CAROL: I can't make it work, it doesn't fit the rhyme scheme.

THERESA: What?

CAROL: I can talk around it, but "Trump" doesn't fit in: O, for whence the race of conservatives come, and the long hands of tax evasion run, their banish'd gods – deregulation, privatisation – restor'd, to May the Orange Supremacists wotsit ador'd. Or would you prefer: I sing of

> expenses and of a Tory, who, forc'd by fate, and haughty Ukip-ian hate, expell'd and exil'd, left the EU block, then tight-lipped, caressed the Republican cock.

THERESA: That'll have to do, as a draft if nothing else – for now. Hopefully they'll all forget.

Theresa picks up a newspaper. The front page is an image of a white advertising van with a provocative poster, black on yellow text reading "In the UK illegally?" and "Go Home Or Face Arrest."

THERESA: Speaking of forgetting, have you heard this? They're being very rude about me. For instance – The Guardian – whatever do they guard, it's not their marbles, *(awkward sighing laugh)*. They said that my "Go Home Illegals" van was a failure. It wasn't – figures show that exactly eleven people left the UK because of my £9, 740 van. Apparently the immigrants are a little miffed. Really, the rich white ones ought to know I wasn't referring to them. Just all the other ones. It's not their country, it's my country. I'm the Prime Minister. And, we text 1500 suspected illegals. True that a thousand of those were sent in error which used up a lot of time for officials to sort through. But that's what they're paid for, to sort my messes. I'm the Prime

	Minister. The country will have to sort my messes, it's how a hierarchy works!
CAROL:	Is there anything else I need to know, to finish this damned thing?
THERESA:	I've had a spat with Scotland. Sturgeon and I aren't seeing eye to eye. It's simply, regarding another independence referendum, it wouldn't be proper to let the Scots make such a crucial decision about the future of my empire. Plus, they don't know anything – they ought to just trust me and keep quiet.
CAROL:	*(with her head in her hands)* Even putting aside that I am Scottish, that double standard, Prime, that doesn't fit the characterisation you're after. In fact, this totally fucks the canon.
THERESA:	Well, you've got to make it work.
CAROL:	Alright: Acne-spotted leopard uses cover-up, foundation her right wing nation, puss. Flys, backwards, strong arms the beebs right, decisions divisive, divided the sheep from the land, rent, bedroom tax, PR hack: buses don't need citations. Breaking news! The emperor has no clothes, but what great legs she's got! Scots don't need their own parliament, to parley's impermanent, refer to me, your

	queen, prime, supreme, May, Theresa – appeased.
THERESA:	What was so hard about that?
CAROL:	Ok, fine. Whatever. Just, before I start writing the next bit, tell me plainly. What is your plan for Brexit.
THERESA:	To deliver a successful Brexit.
TOGETHER:	And Brexit means Brexit.
THERESA:	Precisely. And, post-article 50, I personally select which laws apply in the in Great England, and the others, via my Great Repeal Bill. Once I've sorted that my very next executive order – oh, no, wrong phrase. Donald's been getting to me – my Great Repeal Bill will change the order of the months of the years. You see, Augustus got August, I'm already May – but I can make May first. I deserve it. I'm the Prime Minister. And I'm the leader of a new era, so why not a new year. New year, new EU! What do you think, should that go in the poem?
CAROL:	Uh, can we just go back to the Repeal Bill? So that's what you decide. That becomes law.
THERESA:	Precisely. No fiddling, no transparency malarkey.

CAROL: Okay, uh, so I can – in order to dispute your political opponents, what are some things that've been said against this bill?

THERESA: *(stroppy)* Well Jeremy said I was acting like Henry VIII. Really. Just because I want to set a precedent wherein I frequently determine the law without scrutiny, transparency, or the possibility for reversal – he assumes I intend to behead my husband.

There sounds a BBC news notification. THERESA and CAROL check their phones.

THERESA: Oh no. This again.

CAROL looks accusingly at THERESA, pissed off.

CAROL: You're still selling weapons to Saudi Arabia. While sending medical aid for the victims of those weapons.

THERESA: £85 million in aid, £3.3 billion in arms.

CAROL: So what, that's 3 billion two hundred and fifteen million in profit. How hypocritical can you get? What, supply and demand? They're using UK manufactured bombs to blow up schools.

THERESA: Look, I'm the Prime. That means difficult choices.

CAROL: Who lives, who dies, who profits?

THERESA: No, no. That's not right, that's not how you ought to talk about my decisions. Just, I'm the Prime Minister. If I cannot be loved, then... then they and you are not allowed to have opinions anymore. No use, you'll just do it wrong. I get to do the thinking for this country, not you, not them. I do. And I think that's a good thing. Isn't it a good thing? I said, it's a good thing! Agree with me! Love me! Appease me!

CAROL: You're a glass cliff, love. It's a thing. During times of instability, women finally, at last, get promoted to positions of power. Not so they can fix things, of course, but so they get the blame – and the consequence – for the things that went wrong before their time, punished for men's incompetence, their greatest persecutor is hindsight. And so, back down the cliff we go, inch by inch, mile by mile, descending back to the place they want to put us. And you're part of that now, this system. I have no sympathy for you. Let your legacy be mute. You've done your damage.

THERESA: How dare you?

CAROL: I dare. And I won't be the only one. And in fact, my work, my poems: you don't get them, you don't get to keep them. I'll delete them right now-

THERESA ekes out a villainous laugh.

CAROL: What?

THERESA: Delete? My legacy? Your, ha! Poems. Mine. It's not called the snooper's charter for nothing, love. Your poems were mine the second you started typing. I've privatised your thoughts, your words are stock and I've all the shares. You are owned by money's power, and I've all the political capital I need.

The video call ends. Laughing once again, THERESA faces the audience.

THERESA: I do hope I have your vote on June 8th.

THERESA exits, with a bounce in her step.

Reflection

The intended one-off showing of Emperor May received unanticipated interest and encouragement for a longer edition to be produced for the following year.

At the time of the 10 minute show, the country was gearing up to another general election; this one an attempt to solidify her mandate and appear strong in parliament. (In fact, the original draft was compiled and naively considered finished on April 18th 2017 – hours before May called a snap election. Over the coming days, jokes which had been hyperbolic and future tense were amended to less-satisfying past tense.) Hence, the expanded title highlighting the immediacy of the messages: there're thirty days left between this show and the election. Is this going to be your Prime Minister?

I was inspired by Dario Fo's *The Accidental Death of an Anarchist*, particularly his formula for open hypocrisy and play between performers. Furthermore, I was intrigued by how Fo stayed relevant in a changing political scene: Fo's play was updated each day to reflect the latest news from the nearby courtroom (investigating the death of Giuseppe Pinelli, having been arrested following the Piazza Fontana bombing, as he somehow left the building from the fourth-floor window during a routine interrogation).

So, too, I rewrote the script every day to match the headlines. When A Play About Theresa May was later produced for performance over a longer period, I exhausted myself to include such rapid response theatre. It's a challenge to keep your punchlines and plot arcs relevant in a 24-hour news cycle, when something can change five minutes before the curtain raises; and with smartphones and notifications, the audience is sure to be aware of the news just as soon as you are.

(Or, even better, the performance itself might be how the audience discovers the latest twist in political affairs. What a wonderful way to learn!)

The other aspect of Fo's work which I admire and worked to achieve is the opposition of catharsis to indignation. Catharsis is the idea that arts can purge emotions from the audience, bringing a relief after the stress or thrill of a piece. But cathartic art aims to let off steam, stir thoughts but not necessarily action: performances intending to fuel change have to highlight the capacity for change *and* empower the audience. Indignation can be the fuel for change.

My secondary influence goes back to the Roman Empire, which the privileged English elite ideologically styles itself after. Such exceptionalism (the arrogant idea that we are unique and superior to all others) breeds entitlement to power and dehumanisation of those outside the in-group. I see this at play in the rhetoric of the British National Party, the UK Independence Party, and the Conservative party.

The remaining shadows of the British Empire is aesthetically and philosophically moulded after Ancient Rome and Ancient Greece: idealising conquest and divinity, of slaying giants and dragons and centaurs – that your enemies are filthy foreign monsters – of being born innately more deserving than others, and history itself gets set in beautiful jaw-dropping stone and gold and rubies.

I recalled how Emperor Octavian, later known as Augustus, wanted a poem to rival the stories of Ancient Greece – who had far more involved creation epics than Rome's wolf-suckling fratricide. How could that story inspire a greatness of citizenry and the mandate to expand? How could that story inspire captured nations to bow without a smirk, to assimilate without hate?

And, following a period of crisis where the country's leaders were engaged in a civil war (in our modern case, a Conservative leadership contest) Augustus sought out a poet to produce propaganda in his favour. Virgil's *Aeneid* foreshadows the leadership of Augustus, justifying his recent acts by claiming he had always been fated to be so. It's not known if Virgil agreed with the vision he shared or whether he was strong armed into this creation.

With the inherited Brexit on the horizon, May was forced to create a narrative to compete – and beat – European branding of unity and mingling. Now, the UK has to be *separate* and *better*. Ideally without untangling the union of the four nations.

Augustus had Virgil create a legacy, to tie his acts to pre-ordained and inarguable destiny through Aphrodite's blood, ergo having Zeus' favour.

Theresa May can have the next best modern thing: a poet laureate.

Carol Ann Duffy, of course, is known to not be a fan of the Conservative party. The collection of her poems featured in the national curriculum, *The World's Wife,* were already familiar to me and I used her specific poem *'Politics'* to create a style guide for generating new poems in her tone. Phonic repetitions within a sentence and commas between synonymous words, provoking connections in the audience's mind, as well as twisting popular phrases into relevant metaphors: Duffy's poetry lends itself well to live performance.

I decided that the internal conflicts were between Duffy's morals and her commission, and May's ideological right to rule and her stunning inability to lead. May flits about the stage and about her mind: she leaves, and returns, and has bad ideas on-stage and in the wings. May *must* have the public believe in her and get the marketing power to justify anything she does. Duffy must find a way to end the video call *without* gifting the Conservative Party leader any more power.

A final point of note is that Virgil did not consider the *Aeneid* fit for publication. Before his death, he ordered the manuscript of the *Aeneid* to be burned.

Augustus intervened, however, arranging for the poem to be published against Virgil's wishes.

Given the ongoing turmoil around the "snoopers charter" in which the government would gain unprecedented access to private data, I saw fit to draw another parallel at the invasive nature and entitlement of her leadership.

And, of course, May – like August – is just a month of the year. It passes.

Redirection

On the 644th day of her Premiership, we snuck into the House of Commons to perform an unauthorised showcase on the front benches.

I had revisited the Emperor May script and made the decision to drop the parallel to Virgil's *Aeneid* and May's search for legitimacy to cement her power. (At this point in time, she had won her first <u>public</u> election as leader and had the power she craved.) Now she was spinning in policy circles, laying rhetorical traps and then walking into them. Instead of a poet laureate, I shifted heavily towards physical comedy. Specifically, clowning.

I devised and performed the following edition with Conér Swords, a directing MA grad I knew, who brought his clown know-how. Some scenes began to feel more like a political pantomime and others as skits from the 1984-1996 original series of *Spitting Image*. The Conservative party's commitment to nonsense language, feigning blamelessness around their own bloodied hands, disavowing the hope of anything better – is grotesque.

By this point, May's government had already been likened to a zombie, her countenance to a robot, and her record on disability rights a "human catastrophe" (UN). The plan was to magnify the ugliness of May's government.

I planned for layers of comedy, pairing wit with physical timing, expressions with pose, and an excess of props with a desolate stage. Where the character of May can be pitied or hated, it is the 'character' of the multi-rolling performer who is pitied for being forced – like the public – to live exhausted and exasperated in the same world as Theresa May. The multi-roller is the Everyman.

Much like editing in film can be famed as "if you notice it, it's bad", multi-rolling's typical goal is to perform as the separate roles and not be noticed as a multi-part performer. By not hiding this, it begins to dawn on the audience that the burden on this actor is unbalanced. While May is funny because the character takes herself seriously and still fails, the overworked multi-roller is funny because they cannot avoid failure by working harder or smarter and will suffer with her.

Instead of being drawn into the imaginary world on-stage, the show is a constant reminder of it's falseness and the politics is a constant reminder of its truth. There is no sitting back, unbothered, by what's happening 'over there' on stage when the performers intrude and invade. Unlike the return-to-body after a good film at the cinema, the intention of this show is to constantly feel your feet, the temperature, your breath: to never leave your body. It is immediately relevant at all times.

It was 703 days into her reign when The Play About Theresa May tour began.

Interview with David McCabe Jr

Image description: three white, gender-conforming people sat at a table: Conér on the left, Amie in the middle, and David on the right.

David – Amie, Conér, thank you for being here today. I've kind of got to ask because it's putting me a little bit on edge. Why do you have a script with you?

Amie – As in, why do we have a script right now? Oh, we're not doing planning to do anything in particular [to you].

Conér – He's terrified.

Amie – He is!

David – A little bit. I don't want to mess with people who will randomly walk into… I'll let you describe it in your own words and how you came to the decision to do what you did.

Amie – Do you mean in regards to Parliament, or like existing in general?

David – Oh definitely in regards to the Parliament incident!

Amie – Well, ok. Firstly, it was your idea [Conér]. You pitched it to me: that not only, of course, are we pretending to be clowns – of Theresa May, of her government, and other people of relevance – but we need to do things around bringing that to the public, around bringing that to public spaces and keeping this discussion up about our politicians and the people who lead our country. How do they behave, what do they say, what do they do with the power that we've given them. And the fact that we think their answers are a bit inappropriate. I think one of the main inspirations is this clip of Theresa May laughing in the House of Commons.

David – This one.

Amie – Exactly. That one. And the discussion – I can't remember whether it was to do with more austerity, more recession, more welfare cuts, the hardships caused – and you look across the bench as the camera is angled, and you see the Tory party jeering, shouting, heckling. And Theresa May laughing in the middle.

Conér – Yes.

Amie – Not just does she do these things that cause pain, she seems to be revelling in it.

Conér – She's got the most ridiculous laugh I've ever seen in my life.

Amie – Yes!

Conér – It's obviously, like, performed. A performed laugh. And so you've got to think to yourself 'what are these politicians doing? What are they actually up to?'

Amie – Yeah

Conér – And so I think, I think part of the parliament idea was there's two uses of that place. There's the politics and there's the commercial use. So people go on tours and stuff there, right. When it's during recess in particular – when they take their holidays. And I thought it would be a good idea to sort of palm off the politicians and try to find a loophole – because there's a law about not protesting in the Houses of Parliament, or even outside the House of Commons.

Amie – It's for one kilomile or something. You can't protest –

David – A kilomile? That's a new unit of measurement.

Amie – Something like that! You can't protest in this distance because it's illegal.

Conér – 1Km.

Amie – Yes, that. Whatever that's called.

Conér – Amie speaks in her own measurement. So yeah, I thought it'd be hilarious basically, to creep in to the House of Commons and perform a thing.

Amie – Not *protesting*. To perform.

David – Not a protest, a *performance*.

Conér – Which is what I tried to explain to the head of security. In particular, because she kept on asking *me*!

Amie – Yes!

Conér – She kept on asking me –

Amie – 'What are you protesting! What are you protesting!'

Conér – Why *me*? Everyone just ignored Amie.

Amie – I looked really polite.

Conér – As soon as Amie had done her thing –

David – What was her thing?

Amie – So the actual plan of action when we got there was: a couple of unnamed people *happened* to have cameras on them, because you're also not allowed to record – so it was all an *accident* that any footage occurred.

David – Ok.

Conér – They tried their best.

David – They are in no way affiliated with your play.

Conér – Yeah. They did try their best, security did try their best. They worked out what was going on.

Amie – Yes, the security are absolutely impeccable there. Of the 3 cameras that were switched on in the room, two of them happened to get caught. Almost immediately. So the plan was – I'm wearing the clothes of Theresa May, my costume, underneath a long black coat. For the drama!

Conér – We walked in with our [clown] noses around our necks. It wasn't like we were being subtle.

Amie – I ducked down to make sure no one was looking at me, quickly put on my wig, threw off my coat, and I had to get passed a barrier to get to Theresa May's seat. I got spotted. Like, security guards were definitely tracking me across the room, following my movement. But I got to the seat too fast, sat down, and started cackling. And the fantastic thing is, you can see this in the footage, there are audio tours going on where people wear headphones and walk around as well as a guided tour with a person speaking. There's a guided tour happening right behind the seats and the guy giving the guided tour – I think he's the only person who got offended by what we did. And that is of course he was in love with the House of Parliament, what it stands for, the history. He's taking people around on a tour, that's his job, he must love it.

Conér – He was particularly upset with me.

Amie – Yeah. Oh god.

Conér – Because I sat in the speaker's chair.

David – I heard.

Conér – And I put my feet up.

David – (audibly gasps)

Conér – I was just shouting ridiculous things. Like 'Order!' Oh, and 'You're the most disagreeable Lady'. Something like that. Which, I tried to keep it parliamentary. Then the guard was telling me to get down, so I said 'I don't need to take the advice of some guard.' He was loving it! The guard was loving it.

Amie – All the guards were laughing.

Conér – But yeah, this guide was like…. He looked really disappointed and upset with us as if I just shot his baby.

Amie – What it is - is that the seats where the opposition sit, thing is you're not meant to touch any of the chairs. I do not doubt that someone at some point in history who hasn't been elected has sat on those seats and been told to get out of those seats. I suspect that has happened. People find that offensive, perhaps. Because it is a disrespect to power. And it's a mockery of that power and that position.

Conér – I think it's about having to be elected to sit in that seat, right. But they are just chairs. And a lot of these people in these chairs are in safe seats. No one can do anything about them being there or not being there. Theresa May –

David – Was in that seat for 6 months despite having never been elected.

Conér – Yeah.

Amie – Exactly!

Conér – So in the end, for me, it became more about the performance there than trying to get the footage. What happened there will always stay there. Because of the quality of the footage – the quality being quite bad – it's hard to see what's happening there and even if the quality was good I don't think you'd quite grasp what happened. I've never heard a silence like that.

Amie – Oh no. It was – you know like the whole 'a penny drop' silence. It was almost more deafening than that.

Conér – It was intimidating. It was an intimidating silence. Not only were there like forty, fifty people in the House of Commons itself – there were people, about a hundred to two hundred people in the lobbies.

Amie – And all the doors are open. Everything echoes through the space.

Conér – So you can hear us from the chamber all the way through the House. So people were just watching us and hearing us, the whole place went really quiet.

Amie – Absolutely. And especially because, when we were eventually being led out, we kept on our clown noses. We're proudly in our costume. So people who had heard something had happened, they may have heard my cackle then shouts of 'Order! Order!' then 'Get out of that seat!' 'Order! Order!' 'No, I'm not getting out of this seat.' They see us, and people were taking off their headphones or stopping to look as we passed. And some people were smiling and waving. Some people thought 'eh'. There was one comment that we got on the camera which was someone going 'ugh, drama students!'

Conér – I think someone had asked her what had happened and she went 'amateur dramatics' or something. And the first person went 'aww, I'm sad I missed it.'

David – Alright, so that's really interesting. So the audience, which was an untrained uninformed audience, could recognise that this was a performance.

Amie – Oh, yeah.

David – And *not a protest.* So here's the cutting question: do you think there is actually a difference between a performance and a protest. Do you think a protest is a form of performance?

Amie – I think legally we were not protesting. I think, in the truth of what's going on, if we were not in opposition to what Theresa May is doing, that the Conservatives are doing, if we did not have a feeling of outrage towards them and a need for there to be a change – well this play wouldn't be happening. So we wouldn't have gone there. We wouldn't have done anything. The core desire that has inspired this play is a feeling of protest. Of resistance.

Conér – It is a protest. I mean, your question is an interesting one. Because, is protest a performance?

David – Well, it takes up space. It's a spectacle. Which reminds me: you were mentioning the fact that it was deathly silence in the House of Commons when you were doing this so there is no way of escaping the sound and the spectacle of what you're doing. Do you think this is an essential part of what you're doing?

Amie – It was not a planned part. I think we didn't comprehend how silent it would be nor how still everyone would get.

Conér – Yeah. Or how focused they would be on *us*. Like, I don't know, for some reason I expected people not to care. You know. And for some reason, everyone cared.

Amie – Yeah. I expected the security guards to man-handle us more and I expected the public to care less. And maybe that's a reflection of my views on protest. I see a lot of footage of police brutality – of police pushing back peaceful protesters but letting institutions have, you know, evil power over populations. I'm used to seeing people in authority – security guards, and things like that – as

Conér – The oppressor.

Amie – Yeah, oppressor. The threats to resistance. The threats to protest. Ok, so I thought they're going to come down *harder* on us than they did. And the media has taught people to be quite passive – as a generalisation – so I thought that the people we had captured as our audience, yes they're going on a Saturday to the Houses of Parliament – but is that because they're politically engaged or is that because it's an old building so why not.

Image description: three white, gender-conforming people sat at a table: Conér on the left, Amie in the middle, and David on the right.

Conér – I think though why they called us a performance and not a protest is because we were wearing red noses. We were developed characters. So I feel that there was a mask of... people might have thought it was frivolous, almost. A bit of nothing. A play. Not necessarily a protest against how the politicians, how the MPs perform themselves. We were almost mirroring the way they performed. You go into the

House of Commons on a Wednesday, for PMQs, they're going to sound like fools. The jeers and the way that they talk to each other is borderline ridiculous. It's borderline clown-like. So I feel like the audience thought it was a performance just because they were slightly entertained. They were first confused and then amused. So they were entertained by it. Whereas the security thought it was a protest just because we were in a place that people try to protest a lot. It was interesting. The head of security was so sure we were protesting.

Amie – Absolutely. The head of security had a protocol for 'They're protesting' so make them leave the building. If they admit that they're protesting, we could've been liable for a fine or imprisonment. So her entire thing was Get Them Out Of The Building, Stop Them Causing A Scene, perhaps Get Confession Of Protest out of them.

Conér – But then, as soon as she couldn't get that out of us, kind of realised that we were actually being clowns... Because she wasn't there [during the performance] –

Amie – She didn't see it, she was called to the scene afterward.

Conér – So she thought, as the security and the people in authority thought it was a protest, and after me and her doing this thing of like 'we're not protesters'.

David – 'This is Theresa May!'

Amie – Exactly.

Conér – After that she was like 'If you take off the noses, I'll let you stay.'

David – That's *really* interesting. So if you take off that costume you stop being a protestor.

Conér – Yes, she wanted to strip our -! She thought this was a power. She must've thought that, well, who knows what she thought. But from what I got from her was like after she decided that 'ok, maybe they weren't protesting. They were just doing a performance of some kind.' Like performance art. Which was what we were doing. Performance art in a space where you're not invited to do something in a space. It was the hardest thing to do, in a way.

Amie – It was absolutely terrifying. And I think we both had different emotions about it. I think, going in we were both quite frightened of it. Because, again, going into the Houses of Parliament, they have airport-like staff and security. You can't take liquids, you can't take all sort of things in. Um, we had read all the terms and conditions for what you're allowed to do here. Which, if anything, I think googling the terms and conditions to visiting parliament *that many times* should've been a red flag of my existence.

David – Oh yeah.

Conér – But I feel like, in a way, you could probably get away with more.

Amie – Oh we could've. With hindsight, [I completely agree].

Conér – It was airport security but they didn't care. They weren't really noticing, they weren't looking at you.

Amie – They were scanning you and if you beeped they'd scan you with a different machine. It was very by rote to them. They were very bored. People don't try to do anything because the existence of these employees in that place deters anything from happening.

David – Interestingly enough, they do refer to that as *Security Theatre*.

Amie – Really? I love that.

David – That's another thing I was going to mention. So the security guards, you mentioned how they in all the representations they are a lot more aggressive whereas the footage they tend to show of an audience reacting to protest and performance is a lot more passive. So you could make the argument that security is theatre because they're dressing up in a certain costume, presenting a certain attitude, and having to react to their audience in a way.

Conér – There were definitely different security characters. I was almost glad that we had the good security, because we had a nice security guard actually. You know, he was a nice person. His name's Phillip.

Amie – He was nice.

Conér – He was a nice guy. Honestly, he wasn't really bothered about it. But the other security guard did yell at me and I think if we had had him –

Amie – He would've been much more hands-on. What happened as well was we did the performance, I got asked to leave so I politely left but continued talking and performing. You [Conér] were taken from the [Speaker's] chair because you refused to move when they asked you to. And like I said, the doors are all open. So they take us out of the House of Commons to the Lobby where –

Conér – There's like hundreds of people!

Amie – So the House of Commons was thirty, forty people. They take us to the Lobby where there's like a hundred people and they go 'Stand in this corner'.

Conér – And we were there for like ten more minutes!

Amie – They kept asking for backup [into their shoulders]. 'Where's the – where's the backup we asked for.' And the police aren't coming because the police are probably going 'this isn't worth our time.'

Conér – You could tell that every authority member was like 'what?'

Amie – There was no protocol for us.

David – Which, I'd argue again is a kind of performance. They're keeping you in a public space where you can be watched, where they can make an example out of you.

And they're saying 'more police are coming for you! More police are coming for you!' But they're not.

Amie – My favourite thing that happened. So we're in this naughty corner, as I refer to it, and there's all these other seats we're not allowed to sit on. He [Conér] sits. There's all these busts we're not allowed to touch. Conér touches them. We're told to stay in the corner. He [Conér] leaves the corner. Clowning! But my favourite thing that happened is – we're stood there, waiting for the police, our hearts are still going [fast] because I'm still terrified I'm going to be arrested somehow.

Conér – I know we're not getting arrested.

Image description: three white, gender-conforming people sat at a table: Conér on the left, Amie in the middle, and David on the right.

Amie – He knows, I'm still scared. And there was a blond mum and her young daughter, and they had seen this entire thing go down and when we were taken into the lobby and stood in the corner, they came out. And the mum and the daughter are there, looking at us, and the daughter loudly goes 'What's happening over there?!' and the mum says my favourite thing. She says 'those people sat where they shouldn't have so now they're waiting for the police to take them away.' I found that hilarious. And the thing is they're not that far away. [about two metres] So we can hear them. So I just repeat it back because Conér missed it. They've now heard me repeat it back, they've seen Conér and I laugh about it. The mother is embarrassed. The daughter doesn't know now whose her idol: my mum or these guys. I loved watching that conflict. I loved this whole interaction with the little girl. Because while I'm smiling and waving at her, the mum's like 'Shit, I'm taking her away [from your influence].' So there were all these different little interactions between authority and curiosity.

Conér – That's why for me it was more about the space. It was about saying this was a performance art that belonged to that space in that time with those audience members. Who knows what would happen if we did it again.

Amie – That's something we've both talked about. Because now that we know the layout we could get away with more.

Conér – For sure.

Amie – Oh yeah. The thing is, have they now got a policy about us? Because they didn't. What we did they had no policy for. Now, if it was that big an incident they'll've had to get their managers together to create a policy just for us.

David – If you see any gentlemen wearing a red nose and big trousers –

Conér – Yeah. You know that because it was all very calm and polite at the same time.

David – Very British.

Conér – We weren't too much trouble. They decided we weren't too much trouble.

Amie – The response definitely scaled down. At the start they were calling for police.

Conér – Well, let me clarify, actually. Because you're already in the corner and this guy's holding onto me, brings me to another security guard and this girl that worked there was like 'can you get the police for *this guy*'

David – This guy specifically!

Amie – Not me!

Conér – They decided that you [Amie] were fine and that it was me that should be arrested. Can we just clarify that?

Amie – Oh absolutely. I was very good at going 'I've done what I set out to do, you've told me to stand here, so I'll stand here, but you haven't told me to shut up.' My type of protest, as an individual, is I'm very good at spiteful obedience. Also known as malicious compliance.

Conér – Writing letters and shit.

Amie – So there's civil disobedience where you disobey the law because it's wrong. But then there's obedience to the letter where it's almost malicious. Like if you get told you have to cycle in the cycle lane no matter what's there, but you follow that rule and hit the person who told you to who was walking in the cycle lane. That's a spiteful obedience.

Conér – Probably illegal as well.

Amie – So what I do is go 'Ok, you told me to do something. But you're going to regret having ever told me to do anything because I'll do it in the one way you don't want.' Whereas what you do, Conér, is you get told to stay in the corner and go 'what's the opposite of that?' So we're two very different styles of resistance to authority and their instruction. What I loved as well was when we were eventually getting led out by the head of security, who is engaging with us in conversation – just trying to understand our motives –

David – 'What the fuck am I looking at?'

Conér – Yeah, she was *so* confused.

Amie – One thing I didn't know until we got the footage back is when we were being led from one lobby to another lobby to another lobby to another lobby on our way out – I did notice these two police officers walking towards us and we're led around them. And these two police officers, who had smiled at me and I'd smiled back and waved politely, and I saw them take a double-take because of the nose, the make-up, the hair, we can hear on the tape that just as we've gone passed them they said 'wait! Is that them? The people we're here for.'

David – Wow

Amie – It was just so wonderful to experience a range of reactions that we weren't expecting at all. And I'm excited to see how people respond to the new play.

Image description: three white, gender-conforming people sat at a table: Conér on the left, Amie in the middle, and David on the right.

Data Subject Access Request Ref D18-04

From: Information Rights And Information Security (IRIS) <iris@parliament.uk>
Subject: D18-04 Subject Access Request response

Dear Amie,

I am writing in response to your request under the provisions of the Data Protection Act 1998 (DPA), copied below, which asks for access to the following information:
- A text transcript of the CCTV recording of an incident in the Chamber of the House of Commons on 7 April 2018.
- Still images relevant to the text transcript.
- A list of where information relating to the incident, such as CCTV footage and/or any official documentation is being held.

Following a search for relevant information I enclose the personal data to which you are entitled under the right of data subject access as described in Section 7 of the DPA. This data consists a transcript and two still images. I can also advise you that the CCTV footage and incident report is held in the operational offices of the Parliamentary Security Department (PSD), within the parliamentary estate. This information was collected for the purpose of the administration of justice and supplied for the purpose of your request by the Parliamentary Security Department.

Please note that information which is considered the personal data of a third party has been withheld in accordance with section 7 (4) and 8 (7) of the DPA as release of such data may breach the principles of the Act.

If you have any other queries, please do not hesitate to contact me.

Yours sincerely,
Information Rights Manager

THE PLAY ABOUT THERESA MAY

House of Commons Chamber Incident - 7 April 2018

12:50:11	Data subject (DS) enters chamber with a group of other people. Walks slowly into Chamber to the right of the Speaker's chair.
12:50:51	DS reaches the middle of the Chamber and stops to look around.
12:51:24	After milling around in the crowd, DS walks back to stand close to the Opposition Despatch Box. Appears to talk to a companion.
12:52:04	DS walks forward again across the main floor of the Chamber, looking in her bag.
12:52:19	DS stops by the Bar of the Chamber, pulling what appears to be a card or leaflet out of her bag and looking at it. She then waits, looking down the Chamber, towards her companion standing by the Speaker's Chair.
12:53:26	DS unhooks her shoulder bag and drops it on the floor in a corner at the end of the front bench. She squats down and looks through it.
12:53:40	DS takes a drink from a bottle in her bag.

12:54:10	Still squatting, DS removes her glasses and dons a blonde wig.
12:54:12	DS removes her coat as she stands, dropping it on the floor. She quickly steps inside of the rope cordon by the benches and walks back to the Government Front Bench where she sits on the bench behind the Despatch Box.
12:54:19	Almost immediately she is spoken to by a tour guide standing behind her and she leans back to say something, gesturing with her hands.
12:54:21	DS stands up, gesturing to her companion.
12:54:28	DS is approached by Security Officer.
12:54:35	DS walks past the guard back to where she left her coat and bag.
12:54:56	DS puts glasses back on and picks up her coat and bag from the floor.
12:55:04	DS exits the Chamber, heading towards the Members' Lobby.

THE PLAY ABOUT THERESA MAY

House of Commons Chamber Incident - 7 April 2018

12:52:20 Standing at end of front bench

12:54:11 Removing coat

A Play About Theresa May

Devised by Amie M Marie with Conér Swords

Concept and Text by Amie M Marie

First performed 16th June 2018

Image description: Amie dressed as Theresa May, with blue jacket, chunky necklace, a grey wig, aged make up, and a red clown nose.

A small stage. One cold-white light on the centre, where a broom stands. The broom has a black jacket and NHS badge. At the very back of the stage, a backdrop is hung between two coat stands, with the cloth baring the words "Tory Land of Glory."

A JUNIOR DOCTOR CLOWN enters. Sweeps. Looks around. Then kicks over the broom, and flees from the stage.

CLOWN: Fuck you Jeremy Hunt!

The JUNIOR DOCTOR CLOWN exits.

THERESA MAY enters. She spots the broom.

MAY: Oh, Jeremy, Jeremy. What have they done to you? Who knew doctors – even junior ones – had so much – Oh, Hunty, you flatter me. Come, come.

MAY smiles coyly, and caresses the jacket. The broom is carefully raised to its 'feet', jacket brushed, and gently led away to leave the stage. MAY turns to give speech to the audience, as if at a podium. She clears her throat.

MAY: I follow in the footsteps of a great, modern prime minister. Under David Cameron's leadership, the government stabilized the economy, reduced the budget deficit, and helped more people into work than ever before. But David's true legacy is not about the economy, but about social justice. If you're just about managing I want to address you directly. I know you're working around the clock, I know you're doing your best, and I know that sometimes, life can be a struggle. The government I lead will be driven not by the interests of a privileged few, but by yours. That means fighting against the burning injustice that if you are born poor, you will die on average nine years earlier than others. If you're black, you're treated more harshly by the criminal justice system than if you are white. If you're a white, working-class boy, you're less likely than anyone else in Britain to go to university. If you're at a state school, you're less likely to reach the top professions than if you were educated privately.

The GHOST OF TORY PAST [henceforth 'GOTP'] floats above the backdrop, flapping a bin-bag cape. He makes a howling sound. Pause.

MAY pauses, but does not look.

MAY: If you are a woman,

GOTP enters the stage, sneakily if not for the bin-bag-cape, and howls again. MAY pauses again, but does not look behind her.

MAY: You will earn less than a man.

GOTP howls, louder. MAY looks around but cannot see the source. She continues.

MAY: If you suffer from mental health problems,

GOTP has brought a step ladder on stage. With a loud slam, he places it on the stage. MAY startles at the sound, looks over her shoulder. GOTP freezes. She doesn't see him.

MAY: There's not enough help to hand.

GOTP howls again, now stood on the step ladder. MAY doesn't look. She takes a deep breath in.

MAY: If you're young,

GOTP shuffles the step ladder forward and closer to MAY. He howls. MAY looks the wrong way.

MAY: you'll find it harder than ever before to own your own home.

GOTP howls, very loud and drawn out. MAY finally spots him. She makes a sound of victory. Then confusion.

MAY: Are you on a ladder?

GOTP: No! I'm levitating, for I am the ghost of Tory past!

Silence. GOTP howls again.

MAY: If you're the ghost of Tory past, then where's the ghost of Tory future?

GOTP: He's not here, we can't afford a third person.

BOTH: Austerity.

MAY: That makes sense. So, you come with a message for me?

GOTP: A warning!

MAY: A warning! Oh, I don't like that.

GOTP: I am the Ghost of Tory Past and I bring you a Warning, about Brexit – Brexit means Brexit, not soft Brexit, not flaccid Brexit, but hard, hard, super, missionary, hard, straight down, Brexit. Not a night at the club, doing shots, see a pretty, sexy Brexit, say hi, we're drinking tequila, would you like to come back to mine for some unprotected Brexit?

MAY: Are we doing that or not? I didn't follow.

GOTP: NO! We are not doing that.

MAY: Oh, ok so only a hard, hard, missionary, Brexit, after marriage.

GOTP: No, not after marriage, during marriage.

MAY: Yes, you're right, after would mean a divorce or necrophilia or both, and let's not.

GOTP: I don't believe in divorce anyway. Or abortion.

MAY: Brexit - we need a Brexit!

MAY moves into the audience's space to get an audience member.

MAY: No, not you. No, no. Oh, you'll do!

They return to the stage together.

MAY: How does one marry a concept?

GOTP: On one knee. You need to get engaged first.

MAY: Oh, ok.

MAY kneels.

MAY: What next? Wait, can I ask or should they? What gender is Brexit, is this a lesbian situation?

GOTP: No, Brexit is non-binary

MAY: Even worse. Now what?

GOTP: Say "Brexit"

MAY: Brexit

GOTP: "Will you marry me?"

MAY: Will you – ah, should I wine and dine and woo Brexit first?

GOTP: No. No wine and dine and woo, Brexit is a slut, she knows what she's doing. Hurry up, don't get cold feet.

MAY: Brexit, will you marry me?

GOTP: *(aside)* yes!

MAY: Oh wonderful! You've made me the happiest Conservative.

GOTP: You're not married yet, turn around.

The GHOST OF TORY PAST hums a speedy rendition of Richard Wagner's "Bridal Chorus".

GOTP: Ok, Theresa Mary May, do you take Brexit – British Exit of the European Union, to be your lawfully wedded concept?

MAY: I do.

GOTP: Brexit, do you take Theresa Mary May to be your lawfully wedded concept leader?

The audience member does not get the chance to object.

MAY: You will?

GOTP: Right, now that I've made you do that -

MAY: Wait, made me? Hold on, you look a lot like the MP of North East Somerset? Jacob Reese Mogg?

GOTP: I need to go! The nanny of my eight children is outside and she can't find a parking space, dreadful, dreadful. Fear me! If you fuck this up, I'll be in charge! Long live god, king, and country.

MAY: Ugh, backbenchers.

MAY graciously allows 'Brexit' the audience member to return to their seat. She then resumes her speech.

MAY: As I was saying. We are living through an important moment in our country's history. Following the referendum we face a time of great national change. And I know because we're Great Britain, we will rise to the challenge. As we leave the European Union, we will forge a bold, new positive role for ourselves in the world. And we will make Britain a country that works not for a privileged few, but for every one of us.

TWO PINTS GARAGE [henceforth 'TPG'] bursts in, loud. He has a full pint in each hand.

TPG: Taking back our country, getting back our sovereignty, controlling our borders. Theresa May! Theresa May! I invented Brexit.

MAY: Well-well, Two-Pints Garage! I married Brexit so that makes you my father-in-law, oh god. In any case, as I've made clear

	before, you're irrelevant now. I'm the one who will deliver a successful Brexit for the people.
TPG:	Any Romanians here? Romanians are the worst.
MAY:	They voted remain. Nonetheless, as I've made clear, I'm giving a speech, addressing the public.
TPG:	Yes because you copied me! And since I'm the secret to your success, I've come to tell you something.

TPG passes a drink to MAY. She takes it automatically.

TPG:	Do not, Theresa May, do not be a coward.

TPG lunges towards MAY and results in having an arm around her shoulder. He shakes her at times, giving her a side-hug, and gestures with his remaining pint.

TPG:	Don't be scared of the threats of a hard border between Northern Ireland and the republic. Don't pay a £40 billion divorce bill, though I know you want to – Theresa the Appeaser.

TPG spills some of his drink on MAY and turns away from her, dominating the stage. MAY tries to reclaim the space, but is subverted effortlessly.

TPG:	Ensure no regulatory alignment with the European Union on fishing quotas. Do not

keep us in the single market. Do not participate in some kind of public humiliation whereby you'll have to negotiate on their terms. No transition phase. Remember, no deal is better than a bad deal. If Brexit needs to be fought all over again there will be riots in the streets.

Finally, manic TPG comes to a standstill, MAY positioned behind him, with his arms raised victoriously in the air. The last of his drink lands entirely on MAY.

TPG: See the job through! Make Brexit mean Brexit. You're just like us, Theresa. We're all the same, UKIP and Tories.

MAY: No, I'm not like that.

TPG: Haha, you can't talk! What about the van, when you were home secretary?

MAY: As I've made clear I don't – don't recall any - I couldn't possibly be held accountable for what a van says – freedom of speech, yes? Anyway, it wasn't strong enough – that's why it didn't work. Needed to be more explicit.

TPG: Dear foreigners - "Go Home" Don't be "in the UK Illegally" –Good stuff, May... Oh I need a nap now, I'm sleepy. Bedtime story!

TPG sits on the floor, legs splayed, like a toddler. MAY remains where she is.

MAY: If I say no will you throw your drink at me?

TPG: Yes.

MAY: If I say yes will you throw your drink on me?

TPG: Probably.

MAY sits besides TPG and tells a happy story from memory. TGP drifts off.

MAY: Once upon a time there was a nation that was part of the European Union and after many decades the nation realised that they didn't want to be part of the union. So they all got together and decided by a slim majority to leave. They got out some oars and paddles and moved the country further away and slightly more south so it would be warmer and we wouldn't have to spend money on holidays to France and Germany

TPG: And Spain!

MAY: And we won't have a brain drain to Spain anymore because people will stay here. And our economy will be strong and stable and everyone will be happy and there will be no problems or complaints. The end. Was that ok?

TPG: Very good.

MAY: Are you asleep?

TPG: No, I'm awake.

TPG springs to his feet, leaving MAY on the ground.

TPG: If the government fail and don't deliver Brexit and don't do the job properly and don't get our British passports back, and don't get our fishing waters back, and don't do what seventeen and a half million people voted for then I suppose I'll be forced to come back.

TPG gives one last cheer to the audience and then pours the last pint, the one he gave MAY to look after, over her and then exits the stage.

MAY: We will do everything we can to give you more control over your lives. When we take the big calls, we'll think not of the powerful but you. When we pass new laws, we'll listen not to the mighty, but you. We will – no, this isn't safe. Is there a stage manager or a water manager who can -? Ah, you!

MAY points a finger to off-stage. WORKER CLOWN enters meekly. He is made to clean the stage. He struggles to lift the suddenly-broom and has a woman from the audience help him. They mop together as MAY improv heckles.

MAY: Hurry up, do you want a recession? If you can't do it yourself, outsource it! More labour, more! Just not in the elections!

The stage is sufficiently clean. The CLOWN thanks the audience member profusely and then leaves himself. MAY resumes.

MAY: We will do everything we can to give you more control over your lives. When we take the big calls, we'll think not of the powerful but you. When we pass new laws, we'll listen not to the mighty, but you. We will do everything we can to help anybody, whatever your background, to go as far as your talents will take you. That will be the mission of the government I lead, and together, we will build a better Britain.

MAY sighs. MAY turns away from the audience, tired. MAY gives herself a small slap on the face to stay alert. The Broom is placed on stage, and MAY turns with a huff.

She notices The Broom. She fixes her hair and straightens her clothes out before approaching.

MAY: Oh, Jeremy! I didn't notice you there.

MAY turns her hair between her fingers. She gives a glance up at the Broom through her eyelashes.

MAY: Me? Oh, nothing, thinking out loud. *(beat, laughter)* Oh, you're too kind. *(Affected)* Oh! Jeremy! *(beat)* I suppose -

MAY caresses the jacket, then holds the sleeves as if hands. MAY puppets the Broom.

The music - Send in the clowns, by Judy Collins- plays at a subdued volume. She leans into the Broom's jacket, and looks at peace.

MAY: Oh what a dancer, such a smooth talker. I didn't know you were so talented.

MAY is dipped by the Broom, one leg high in the air.

MAY: No, I would never fire or reshuffle you into a different role- so, you can be honest to me.

The jacket's hands slip down to MAY's lower back. MAY is enthusiastic.

MAY: Oh, Hunty. Privatise these lips, impose an unethical contract on me, squeeze my budget -

MAY places the Broom's sleeve on her chest. Gives a squeeze.

MAY: Push me to breaking point! Hunty!

The DAILY MAIL [henceforth 'MAIL'] walks on. MAY freezes.

MAY: It's not what it looks like.

MAIL shrugs, opens a newspaper. MAY chucks The Broom off-stage.

MAIL: I think you should call an election.

MAY: What? No.

MAIL looks closely at the newspaper. Hmms. MAY rushes to look over MAIL'S shoulder, to see the news.

MAIL: I think you should call an election.

MAY shakes herself, and tries very hard to not look at the newspaper.

MAY: No, my government is exceptionally stable and I have a job to do. Bringing about -

MAIL chuckles. MAY rushes to see why. MAIL takes a step forward, and MAY follows. They begin a "walking holiday" set up, turning in circles around the stage.

Following MAIL, MAY continues her thoughts.

MAY: Bringing about Brexit for the just about managing. Thus, I –

MAIL pauses. MAY nearly crashes. Stumbles over her words.

MAY: - do not think that's a wise decision.

MAIL continues their circle. MAY follows immediately. MAIL stops again, then looks back at MAY. MAY does her best to look innocently occupied with the empty stage.

MAY: What?

MAIL: I think you should call an election.

MAY: I don't see why I —

MAIL: Call. An. —

MAY: What? What does it say? Does the paper, the press… the public, like me?

MAIL looks closely at the newspaper. Scoffs. MAY is unsure. MAIL sets off on his route again. This time with a sillier walk.

MAY: What? What?! Tell me what it is saying about me? Tell me. Am I loved? Am I strong enough? Tell me now!

MAIL stops. Shrugs.

MAY: Will it go well for me, do you think?

MAIL: Call an election.

MAIL winks.

MAY: Will I win it? No, this is a bad idea. A very bad idea. Or perhaps a very good idea. What do you think? Should I call an election? Should I not call an election? Are you on my side? Will you help me if I call an election? So you think I should? Or do you not think I should?

MAY enters the audience and asks for shaking heads and nodding heads. MAY selects an audience member and brings them onto the stage. She puts them between her and MAIL. MAIL sets off again on their walk, the audience member compelled to follow, and MAY takes up the rear.

MAIL: Call an election.

MAIL walks faster. He encourages the audience to join the chant.

MAIL: Call an election!

MAIL walks faster. Gets louder.

MAIL: Call an election!

MAIL walks comes to a stop.

MAIL: Call an election.

MAY: I'll win it?

MAY checks with the audience member, as MAIL nods vigorously.

MAIL: Call. An…

ALL: Election!

MAIL returns the audience member to their seat then exits, victorious.

MAY stands as if at a podium.

MAY: I shall be calling for a general election to be held on the 8th of June. I decided this while on a walking holiday.

An idea occurs to MAY. She grabs two stackable chairs from the wings and sets them up in the space. She hates it. She moves them again. She hates it. She rearranges the chairs entirely.

MAY: Last summer, after the country voted to leave the European Union, Britain needed certainty, stable and strong leadership,

She hates it. She moves them again. She hates it.

MAY: And since I have become prime minister I have delivered exactly that. Despite predictions of immediate financial and economic danger, we have seen growth that has exceeded all expectations.

She hates it. She moves them again. Nothing is going well.

MAY: Britain is leaving the European Union and there can be no turning back. But the other political parties oppose it. Our opponents believe because the government's majority is so small, that our resolve will weaken and that they can force us to change course. They are wrong.

She moves them again. She steps back, and finally seems to agree with their position.

MAY: It will be a choice between strong and stable leadership in the national interest, with me as your prime minister, or weak and unstable coalition government.

The speech ends. MAY looks around.

MAY: Shit. What have I done?

MAY exits. HACKMAN enters. Sits on one of the seats. When no one joins him on stage, he places an apple on the chair opposite him and then slouches back.

HACKMAN: Hello. My name is Jeremy Hackman and tonight we will be exclusively, live from the studio, speaking with Theresa May:

MAY uses the step ladder to peer over the backdrop. She eats chips in a hideous, nervous manner. There is a long pause and an intense look at the apple.

HACKMAN: When did you realise that you had made the wrong decision about Brexit?

Pause.

HACKMAN: Why did you originally believe it was a bad idea to leave the European Union?

Pause.

HACKMAN: You say you went into politics to help the 'just about managing' but how are you

> helping them when you're reducing taxes to help the rich?

Pause.

HACKMAN asks the audience if they have a question, then faithfully asks the apple that question. Silence.

HACKMAN: Right, well, have you changed your mind on Brexit? Have you, changed your mind, on Brexit? BREXIT??

HACKMAN has lost it. He lunges at the other chair. He bites the apple. May gasps.

MAY: Did you just eat me?

HACKMAN: Yes?... Wait?

MAY ducks down. HACKMAN shrugs, and takes another bite. He leisurely leaves the stage, taking a chair with him.

MAY jumps into full view. She scoots the second chair off-stage. She is alone again.

MAY: I'm not interested in interviews. I would like to talk to the people directly. Vote for me! Vote for me. I can count on you.

MAY moves into the audience space, and begins to give out flyers in the Conservative colours and font. They read 'Austerity for Life' 'Disables Are Faking' 'Kill The Poor' 'Brexit Means Brexit' 'No Rights For You' 'Worship The Wealthy' 'Strong And Stable' 'Only Communists Disagree' 'More Bombs Abroad' 'Immigrants Are Bad'

'Close The Libraries' 'Take Back Control' 'Protecting Tory Interests' 'Bold, New, Positive' 'No Magic Money Tree' 'Fear The Red Terror'. MAY improvises around audience reactions.

MAY: No need to read these, just tick the box to vote me in.

DIM BEE makes the sounds of Big Ben bongs.

DIM BEE: *(off)* And the election results are in!

MAY scrambles back to the stage, scattering the remaining flyers.

DIM BEE: *(off)* And what the exit poll is saying is the Conservatives… are the largest party!

MAY celebrates unflatteringly.

DIM BEE: *(off)* Note, they don't have an overall majority at this stage. 314 for the conservatives, that's down 17. The Conservative majority has decreased and at this rate-

DIM BEE leaves the stage by this point.

DIM BEE: *(off)* Theresa May, will have to resort to a hung parliament.

MAY: Shit.

DIM BEE: *(off)* She is expected to resign in the morning.

MAY returns to the stage.

MAY: No, no I'm not. I can make this work.

YE OLDIE QUEENIE WITH HER CORGI [henceforth 'QUEEN'] enters. This startles MAY.

QUEEN: Who's there? Are you a servant?

MAY: Of a sort, yes, but -

QUEEN: Who are you?

MAY: I'm the Prime Minister, I have been and I still am, and I hope I can still be.

QUEEN: Oh, Margaret Thatcher!

MAY: You really see her in me? I'm touched.

QUEEN: Are you not her? Isn't she still –

MAY: No, I'm Theresa May.

QUEEN: Oh. Who was the nice chap, the man before –

MAY: David Cameron

QUEEN: - Nice man

MAY: Not to pigs... can I be prime minister?

QUEEN: Every prime minister must pass a series of tests .... Stroke the corgi

MAY: Shoot the corgi?

QUEEN: Stroke the corgi

MAY: Oh, I'm glad I didn't just do it. Will it bite? Yes. O-oh.

QUEEN: Yes. Good. The corgi doesn't like you, doesn't approve.

MAY: Did I pass the test?

QUEEN: No. But there are more.

The corgi-plushie barks again.

QUEEN: It's a reoccurring joke. The Second test – Woosh my cape. Woosh my cape.

MAY: Woosh your cape?

QUEEN: Yes.

MAY does so. It looks fantastic. A Titanic-esk musical rift plays.

QUEEN: The tiebreaker is …. Would you like to be prime minister?

MAY: Yes.

QUEEN: Alright then.

MAY: Is that it? Pretty sure, last time we met, you asked to see my "true form"?

QUEEN: Yes. I could have said yes at any moment, this was all a game, just lies.

MAY: Oh.

QUEEN: Tu-rah!

MAY: That was a short scene. Really worth the money we spent on the costume.

QUEEN: Bye-bye, May was good seeing you again, always falling for the same jokes. Remember do not turn your back on me.

MAY: Is that a threat or a custom?

The QUEEN shrugs, exits, and leaves behind her corgi.

There is a tense moment as MAY waits for the corgi to attack her again. When it doesn't happen, MAY sneaks forward on the corgi – then kicks it off the stage. Hard.

Overjoyed, MAY does a victory dance.

MAY: I'm Prime Minister again. Officially. Wonderful. Now, I need an ally – if I don't have the EU, I will need an ally. You might say I need someone special that I can have a relationship with. I'll arrange a meeting with -

TRUMP enters.

TRUMP: AMERIKKKA!!

He forcibly holds MAY's hand. MAY tries to pull away, but is tethered. The performers recreate the famous tableau of the pair coming out of the White House together. After a beat, TRUMP tries to lick MAY's face – using their joined hands for leverage.

MAY: Mr. Trump, no means no. Now go. Shoo.

MAY throws TRUMP backstage.

MAY: GAH, Americans… So I cannot rely on them, I'll have to look at, closer to home.

MACRON enters. Despite the exertion of the following, their voices remain sombre and unstrained.

MAY: Ah, Macron. I've been meaning to have a conversation with you.

MAY shakes MACRON's hand.

MACRON: Non.

MAY: Oh, did you not understand my meaning?

They cannot stop shaking hands. It seems they're stuck with each other.

MACRON: Non.

MAY: This is technically blocking but I can work with this… Can we negotiate-?

MACRON: NON.

MAY: Can I have a transition period of 2 to 3 years?

A tug of war breaks out, neither able to get free.

MACRON: Oui. *(Shrugs)*

MAY: Oh, are you sure?

MACRON: Non.

MAY: Right.

MACRON: Oui.

MAY: If we do not get what we want, we may need to put up a hard border between Northern ireland and the Republic?

MACRON: Non, non, non.

MAY: Fine, we won't do that. Can we discuss Fishing quotas in British waters?

MACRON: Non.

MAY: Scandalous, Fine. What about UK nationals in the EU, will the same rights as before?

MACRON: It is all up to you, madame.

MACRON exits.

MAY: UGH, the bloody French... You're blocking the will of the British people, you realise! By being difficult! *(beat)* RIGHT!! I'm calling a cabinet meeting to sort all this mess out. I, and consequently the conservative party, needs to think this through!

MAY begins to yell. The two performers scurry and arrange three chairs side to side, with the seats facing upstage, and the backs of the seats closest to the audience. They crouch behind the chairs. BORIS JOHNSON [henceforth 'JOHNSON'] is there.

MAY: CABINET! CABINET! CABINET!

JOHNSON plays with a bus figurine, running it across the chair seat.

MAY: As some of you are aware, there has been an election. And they voted – wrong – yet they voted.

JOHNSON: The wheels on the bus go round and round, round and round, round and round.

MAY: Not if the bus is stationary, wheelless or falling off a cliff, Boris. There are exceptions to every rule.

JOHNSON: The wheels on the bus go round and round, round and round, round and round.

MAY: Stop with your buses! First the new London buses, then the promise bus! Stop! I never want to hear that word again.

JOHNSON makes incomprehensible sounds. He crouches down, out of sight, and AMBER RUDD [henceforth 'RUDD'] appears in his place.

RUDD: Well I think we should, while we're all in one place, discuss the Windrush generation and the hostile environment towards –

MAY: Do you need a cough sweet, RUDD? You're not sounding like yourself. *(aside)* that's a reference to a conference I've yet to attend. *(as before)* We're talking about the results!

RUDD: *(she turns towards the broom)* What do you think, Jeremy?

RUDD changes wigs and becomes JOHNSON.

JOHNSON: The wheels on the bus go round and round-

MAY: Boris

JOHNSON changes wigs and becomes RUDD.

RUDD: What a fool!

RUDD changes wigs and becomes JOHNSON.

JOHNSON: Why don't you be quiet Amber, no one cares what you think.

JOHNSON changes wigs and becomes GOVE.

GOVE: This is the problem with experts, no one trusts us… Once, I could have been Prime minister but the 1922 committee…

MAY laughs loudly.

MAY: I am sorry, does the Environmental Secretary have some policies to add?

GOVE changes wigs and becomes JOHNSON.

JOHNSON: The wheels-

MAY: Boris! Stop with the bus! You are all so devoid of any policy ideas... I have to call a reshuffle!

Everyone runs away. The chairs are swept off-stage.

Only MAY and the Broom remains.

MAY is coy, flirtatious as before – but now with a side of regret and hesitation.

MAY: Don't cry. Jeremy. Oh, don't look at me like that.

MAY reaches out to the Broom, then sweeps into his arms.

MAY: We must never speak of it. No. Hunty, I can't. As I've made clear, we have other things to discuss. Like, your role as Health Minister. No – don't. Don't cry, Hunty.

MAY uses one of the Broom's sleeves to wipe away his tear. MAY turns to walk away, but is held onto by the Broom. She looks back. She closes her eyes. This is so hard for her to say.

MAY: Hunt, don't. I can't look at you. We can't keep going like this, it's not – it's not right, as I've made clear, and the country expects changes.

WORKER CLOWN enters.

MAY: It isn't, what it looks...

MAY reflexively goes to push away the Broom, denying her affections, but pauses – no longer guilty – and confronts the intruder.

MAY: Oh, fuck it. What do you want?

WORKER CLOWN points a gun at MAY.

MAY: Security?!

WORKER: We haven't got security, remember – we couldn't afford any more cast members.

BOTH: Austerity

WORKER: Right. I have had enough, what are you going to offer me?

There's a pause. MAY squints at the WORKER. She pulls out a Pepsi can, and offers it in the style of Kendall Jenner. There is an awkward beat. The gesture is rejected. MAY tries again.

MAY: In terms of... Policy?

WORKER: Yes!

MAY: Okay, hmm, well, what about, right, what about free school meals for all primary school children?

WORKER: I am not asking for another U-turn!

MAY: Right, what about a fall in tax for low income workers?

WORKER: Go on.

MAY: I will lift the cap on in-work benefits if you calm down!

WORKER: You calm down!

MAY: I don't have gun.

WORKER: I don't have gun.

A beat. The WORKER clearly has a gun. They give each other a confused look.

MAY: Right.

WORKER: I want universal income, free education for all and a real chance for people like me on minimum wage to get on the property ladder.

MAY: I can't do that! *(beat)* LOOK! Karl Marx is over there…

WORKER: Where??

MAY grabs the gun with ease.

MAY: Ah, I won't give you anything. No, in fact you'll do what I want. Leave your Union, don't vote, forget about Grenfell, shut up about the Windrush scandal, ignore the poor, look the royal wedding-!

The WORKER nearly looks.

WORKER: I refuse!

MAY levels the gun at the WORKER.

WORKER: Don't shoot!

MAY fires the toy gun, it flicks out a small red banner with the text 'BANG!'

MAY: Well, that was useless.

WORKER: That was aggressive.

MAY: Do you think you can do a better job?

WORKER shrugs.

WORKER: I don't know. Maybe any of us could.

MAY: Well, of course you can't - because you are not qualified. You deserve to be where you are. As poor, rundown, hopeless as you are. My parents deserve their wealth, I deserved to be born into it, and I am qualified to lead this country out of the EU. More qualified than any of you. So what if it all goes off cliff, if we get no deal? No one can do it better than me.

WORKER exits. MAY sneers at the audience, who did not step in to side with her.

MAY: Till the next election, I'll see you all in Brussels.

Review

There was a choice involved at the end of the show: whether we returned as performers to the stage to bow, allowing for a cathartic breath and closure to the questions raised–or to simply vanish into the changing rooms and let the audience conclude that they ought to leave–aka to do something. The latter reinforced the plan to remove as many barriers between the messages and the bodily reality of the audience; by opting to drop a traditional congratulatory moment, the show gained another chance to provoke thought, choice, and action from the viewer.

While this was not a Boalian show, I continue to be inspired by the Theatre of the Oppressed. Boal's work is often simplified as shows which bring the audience on stage to practice social change. For instance, audience members will replace an actor in the performance and show how they might try to fix a problem, only to see how the reaction of authority changes and traps them again. Sometimes the rehearsal for change succeeds–and the domestically abused, downtrodden worker, forced-marriage child, or honour victim or FGM susceptible can uncover their way through this safe, open forum to escape harm in their life and invent an action for positive change.

By involving the audience and encouraging them to remain within their bodies–rather than swept by imagination into the narrative of a show 'over there' on stage—we keep them rooted in the fact that these injustices are real and relevant and require action.

While none of us knew what the future held, these shows continue to offer a snapshot of opinion in history. While Cameron, May, and Johnson have each inspired a different flavour of indigence, rage, and pain— their contempt for the safety and joy of each of us was shared.

This work was both a personal challenge to test my logistical, event planning, and marketing skills—and a rejection of the politics of our nation. The poor are poor because our Conservative government lets people suffer: the rich are rich because the Tories protects their wealth and power to our disadvantage. Every demographic of innocence and strife has been scapegoated, hate crimes excused in the vitriol spat by untouchable silver-spoon politicians. Our rights as civilians are watered down more and more in the name of the great <u>economy</u>—a false thing benefiting few—when we're really a <u>society</u>.

We have all the technology our ancestors couldn't imagine and all the wealth of our empire past. There's no excuse for the state of Britain. Yet people are allowed to be homeless, allowed to starve, allowed to be excluded and hated and harmed—all because of an ideology that says *some* people have to be superior or what's the point of life?

This ideology says the poor deserve to be poor, and the disabled deserve to die. This belief says that the foreigner should be banished and the workless sent to work camps. That the rich are born worthy and our lives are nothing but numbers spinning their economy wheel.

In our current structure, no one can work to move themselves into financial security and a lifestyle of dignity. Our working class is an overworked class, stamped down and filled with notions of a cosmic-conservative-right to a 'strong' economy at the expense of what makes us human.

When faced with a parody of governance, a realisation must float to the service: the Conservative dream is a lie. Whatever you believe is possible—your own vision of a viable utopia- is worth working towards.

This is not the best we can be.

NORWICH EYE REVIEWS 'SCRATCH IT' AT THE NAC

By Julian Swainson, The Norwich Eye, May 8th 2018

Hack Theatre together with Norwich Arts Centre have hit upon a great formula for an interesting evening of lively and innovative theatre. 'Scratch It' is theatre in development – we are not seeing polished performances that have been rehearsed until the life is squeezed out of them, but work in progress. It is fascinating and gives an unusually frank insight into the way that good theatrical works come to life.

This is all good, but I would admit to being slightly unprepared for an evening which kicked off with me being marched to the small stage to both impersonate Brexit and then be married to Theresa May by a grisly Mogg-alike figure. The capacity audience were polite enough to give me a generous round of applause as I slunk back to my corner seat to try and make some sense of my new marital status, but I soon relaxed into appreciation of the sheer joy of this evening of theatrical talent emerging.

This first work that risked my contribution was called 'A Play About Theresa May' and was both topical and clever, with Amie M Marie giving an uncannily nuanced version of our current Prime Minister albeit with a clown nose. The play will be performed again at the Puppet Theatre on 16th June and I strongly recommend your attendance. Conér Swords wpas the Mogg clown, amongst other roles. Amie had obviously studied some of the real May's facial tics and gestures, which greatly amused the audience.

REVIEW: SCRATCH IT! AT THE NORWICH ARTS CENTRE

by Lewis Martin, The Norwich Radical, May 11th 2018

On Sunday 6th May I attended Scratch It! hosted by Hack Theatre at the Norwich Arts Centre. Aimed at attracting new writers and ongoing projects, the evening looks to give a platform to work that is happening in the area so it can be developed and flourish. The arts varied across the evening, ranging from comedy to drama and using different styles and formats.

The night opened with A Play About Theresa May. In the latter stages of its development, the satire showed Theresa May detailing to the audience her plans for Brexit in a speech. Whilst trying to do so she was haunted by the 'Ghost of Tory Past' in the form of Jacob Rees-Mogg, as well as being ridiculed by 'two pints Garage', a comically dressed Nigel Farage. The play was fantastically set up, focusing on the issues that went further than just Brexit whilst also getting the audience involved, including a member being proposed to so she could 'marry Brexit'.

It will be performed at the Puppet Theatre in June and is well worth a watch.

Amie M Marie is a queer and disabled comedian, writer, and performer with a first class BA (Hons) in Performance and Scriptwriting from the University of East Anglia. Directly affected by right-wing policies on education, environment, welfare, queer rights, and disability safety, her voice is a call to arms to improve the world we inhabit.

Finalist for the Snoo Wilson Award © in 2018 for her research and writing on the callous assessments of disabled people in the UK.

If you want to know when her next books, plays, and performances will appear, please visit her website www.amiemarie.co.uk where you can sign up to receive an email when she has her next release.

www.ingramcontent.com/pod-product-compliance
Lightning Source LLC
LaVergne TN
LVHW051225070526
838200LV00057B/4613